M000233392

Thank You for your Order.

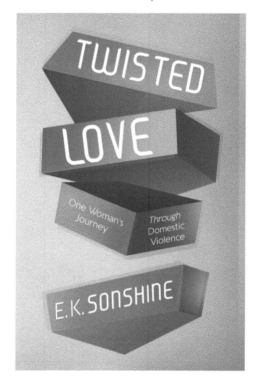

Please tell Family, Friends & Associates!

Paperback $14.95 Ebook $4.95
www.queenzunite.com

KP PUBLISHING COMPANY
Publisher of Fiction, Nonfiction, and Children's Books
24307 Magic Mountain Pkwy, #386. Valencia, CA 91355
661-513-0308 www.kp-pub.com

7/28/2021

Mr. T., I hope you find my book Inspiring, empowering, faith-based and a whole lot of drama :)

Love,

E.K. Josephine

TWISTED LOVE

One Woman's Journey
Through Domestic Violence

E.K. SONSHINE

KP PUBLISHING COMPANY

ISBN: 978-1-950936- (Paperback)
ISBN: 978-1-950936- (Ebook)
Library of Congress Control Number: Pending

Editor: Renee Aldrich
Cover Design & Photography: Juan Roberts, Creative Lunacy
Interior Design: Jennifer Houle
Literary Director: Sandra L. Slayton

Published by:
KP Publishing Company
Publisher of Fiction, Nonfiction & Children's Books
Valencia, CA 91355
www.kp-pub.com

Printed in the United States of America

*"It took me a long time to develop a voice,
and now that I have it, I am not going to be silent."*
—MADELEINE ALBRIGHT

I dedicate this book to my mother's memory. She was a true woman of God who kept me strong during one of the most difficult and traumatic times of my life. May she continue to rest in heaven. And to my father, who had to make the difficult decision to keep me protected while I was yet a vulnerable child.

This work is also dedicated to each person dealing with domestic violence or any abuse—remember, you deserve better.

CONTENTS

CHAPTER 1: The Beginning   1

CHAPTER 2: Early Life   7

CHAPTER 3: Stability   11

CHAPTER 4: Life Changes and Coping Mechanisms   13

CHAPTER 5: Cloudy Days   17

CHAPTER 6: Honeymoon Period Mike and Valerie   21

CHAPTER 7: The Games Begin   29

CHAPTER 8: Physical Abuse Begins   39

CHAPTER 9: On Again, Off Again   53

CHAPTER 10: Victory   63

CHAPTER 11: The Aftermath   69

Epilogue   *79*
Afterword   *81*
Action Steps to Cultivating Your
    Personal Empowerment   *83*

Resources   *87*

CHAPTER 1
THE BEGINNING

Mike put his foot down, "I'm coming to meet your parents tonight."

Valerie felt her stomach turn into knots, her head was throbbing, and she became extremely anxious. She was deeply concerned about how her parents would respond to Mike. Valerie loved him but was well aware of his darker side, which included a possessiveness unfamiliar to her. It was for this reason, among other things, that up to this point, she had been avoiding introducing him to her parents.

They had been together just about six or seven months now, and they were spending a great deal of time together. Valerie had met his mother already, who already loved her. But, still, she was reluctant to introduce Mike to her parents.

There was a change occurring so fast in Valerie's life; it left her head spinning. Beginning with getting a job she loved, then her decision to move out of her parent's home and being on her own, to her first apartment with her friend, Sheila, then that *one-afternoon* meeting Mike, to now. It seemed that overnight he was her everything. She still thinks of the day she met him during her lunch hour.

Valerie was an office assistant for a local real estate office. She loved the sense of independence she had as a result of her work. It took a lot for her to gather the courage to "fly the nest," so to speak, from her parent's home, and this job enabled her to do it.

Given everything she had been through in her life, it felt good being on her own.

The afternoon she met Mike, she was hurrying out to lunch—she had been thinking about lunchtime all morning and was ready for it. She decided to eat at the local hamburger stand across the street from her office. Though she knew she should get a salad, their burgers were to die for. Valerie ordered and picked up her cheeseburger and fries combo and headed back across the street to work to enjoy her lunch.

As she approached her building, she noticed a very "pimped-out" fancy car making a U-turn right before her. As she stepped up on the curb, out of this nice car came an extremely handsome, muscular, sexy man, and he was FINE. His smooth skin, slim nose, and beautiful hair sent her into a lustful tailspin.

These reactions came from a girl raised in the Pentecostal church and who was also still a virgin at 27-years old, but she was still human. She may not have known what it was to have "been with" a man, but Valerie definitely knew what it was to be physically attracted to one.

By the time she stepped onto the curb, he was out of his car staring at her.

"Hi . . . I'm Mike."

On her own, to her first apartment with her friend, Sheila, then that *one* afternoon meeting Mike, to now. It seemed that overnight he was her everything. She still thinks of the day she met him on her lunch hour.

Valerie was an office assistant for a local real-estate office. She loved the sense of independence she had as a result of her work. It took a lot for her to gather the courage to "fly the nest," so to speak, from her parent's home, and this job enabled her to do it. Given everything she had been through in her life, it felt good being on her own.

She felt somewhat self-conscious standing there with this food in her hand and hearing him compliment her on the way she looked. But she felt really flattered when he said *he wanted to get to know her better.*

She had to admit, she enjoyed being complimented, especially considering the fact that she had not been on a date in a long while. But her number one rule was she was not giving out her number—so, it worked out great when Mike handed her his business card.

Valerie went back into work still thinking about how fine Mike looked. She considered him sexy, her type to the T. As she walked back into her building, her co-worker, who had observed her and Mike, asked, "Who was that?"

"Mike," Valerie replied.

"He was really handsome," she said.

Valerie nodded.

"He's mighty buffed. I bet he works out."

She was correct of course, Mike stood at about six feet, four inches tall, I surmised, and looked to weigh about two hundred and fifty pounds. Valerie had to admit his stature was a bit intimidating, especially for her small frame. But she couldn't stop thinking, *this man is FINE. Maybe a little too fine for me, and too flashy as well.*

She finished her lunch while she looked at his business card before she threw it in the trash.

A few days passed and she still could not get Mike out of her head. She regretted throwing away his business card. But at the same time Valerie was actually proud of herself for resisting temptation. This guy had trouble written all over him, she felt, and inside herself she didn't feel comfortable about a possible connection with him—she wasn't sure why she just didn't.

Today work seemed crazier than ever. The phones were ringing off the hook with complaints, business calls, and some personal ones. Valerie talked to a friend of hers for about ten minutes when another call came in. She knew she had to take the call. Valerie answered the phone, and a somewhat familiar voice was on the other end. The caller asked for her by name, and she knew for a fact it was the same guy that approached her two days prior.

She answered, "This is she."

Valerie was both flattered and a little angered that he had the audacity to call her without her permission since she never gave him her number.

He asked, "When were you gonna call me?"

She was caught off guard by the question, after all she had thrown the card away. She made up some answer about being busy during the day, and then having to help her parents in the evening. He didn't know she had thrown his number away the same day he gave it to her. After further thought, she concluded that she was extremely impressed by his persistence and it sent her ego up a couple of notches.

Valerie left work that day on cloud nine! She couldn't wait to share her phone call she received with her roommate.

"So, guess who called the office today?"

"No, I couldn't, so don't make me guess."

"Girl, it was the man from the other day, that Mike."

"Wait, did you give him your work number?"

"Nooo, that's the point, I didn't. And you know what, I threw his number away, and after lunch the phones were ringing off the hook. I answered and he was on the line asking for me—can you believe it?"

"Girl he really wants to get with you, if he's doing all of that . . . talk to him."

That night, Valerie slept like a baby as her thoughts were all about him.

It was eight months ago, and they were now in a full-on relationship even though there were still many strange things about him that had her unnerved, she was still reluctant to take him to meet her parents, even though her heart was completely captivated.

Valerie wanted to go ahead and take him to meet her parents, and he was definitely not happy with how she had been putting it off—and truthfully in her heart knew she couldn't hold out much longer, just waiting for the right time.

It felt odd to her that in just a short time, he seemed to have a great deal of power over her. She completely believed that their feelings for each other were mutual. He was handsome, drove a nice car, and sexually they were a perfect match. Just the thought of making love with him, caused her body to quiver. Yes, they definitely had chemistry. With his skills as a lover, their sex life was at an all-time high. She always burned for him. The conflict within her, however, was real. Even with all this, her inner gut told her there was something to be cautious about regarding his controlling nature. Also, it was his basic environment— the car, clothes, jewelry, his mysterious comings and goings, her unclear understanding about his source of income—it all screamed "drug dealer." Little did Valerie know that her instincts were right on point. In the meantime, however, she had no idea how much her life was about to change, that she would be subjected to mind games, lies, deceit, and even danger—as he was slowly becoming an every-day part of her life. And all the while, though she felt a slight fear, she welcomed it at the same time. He seemed to be the missing link from her life.

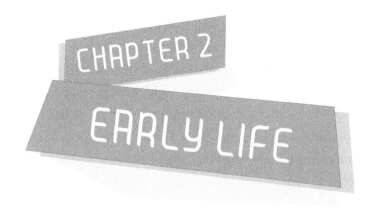

CHAPTER 2
EARLY LIFE

Valerie had been raised by her father and her stepmom, Mary. She loved her family including her extended family. And though her early years were filled with upheaval and uncertainty, she could still see that she had a village. During this time—the time before her dad married Mary—she spent time living with a number of family members. Of these, was a favorite aunt with whom she lived the longest just prior to transitioning to a permanent home with her dad and her stepmom. She really loved living with Aunt Claudia, her dad's sister, where overall life seemed like a barrel of fun. As a result, she maintained many great memories of living with her cousins She had loved the daily picnics, dance offs, and taking many short vacations, and riding in her aunt's station wagon. For her, these felt like the good old days.

With all the goodness surrounding her, Valerie had deep concerns about her birth mother's absence from her life. As a child she couldn't understand why it seemed that her mother did not want her. The questions she asked herself included, *"Why was she living with other family members? Was there something wrong with her?"*

Her dad would take her to visit her birth mom whenever she asked him. He was careful to never speak negatively to her concerning her birth mom. Instead, he always encouraged her by saying, "That's your mom, and she brought you into this world, always respect her."

The older she got, the more it bothered her about her birth mom. She kept wondering, *why she didn't live with her "real mom"* as this stayed on her mind daily. She even began envying her friends, and the relationships they had with their mothers as struggled to understand why she didn't live with hers. As time passed, she began to understand why her dad took her and she understood that the decision he made was in her best interest.

Valerie's birth mother struggled with drugs and alcohol. She had been declared unfit to care for her child. Though it helped to be able to finally get a reason she never lived with her birth mother, the negative outcomes of feelings of rejection and having that sense of abandonment did not leave her. And while not having memories of any physical abuse from her birth mom, she definitely remembers being neglected, and various aspects of the neglect—like times when there was little to no adult supervision, times of inadequate food, and no affection or attention. Valerie never even saw a baby picture of herself. This really troubled her and served as confirmation that she was completely not wanted, after all, who doesn't have a picture of their baby? These things left her feeling deeply unloved, though she ultimately understood what was going on with her mother.

After the marriage, her life slipped into a normalcy that Valerie had not experienced before. She was provided a better sense of well-being, albeit, short lived.

By the time Valerie was five years of age, she was precocious and had a zest for life. She loved her family life, including three siblings, however, she had an early excitement for school and was anxious—even for kindergarten. She excelled there, loved reading, and was asked to participate in several holiday programs because she read on a third-grade level.

Valerie's stepmom, Mary, was patient, loving, kind, and a caring "replacement mom"—and immediately after the marriage, Valerie stopped referring to her as her step- mother. Mary treated her as a mother would and Valerie loved it—so Mary became Valerie's "mother."

Mary was also a seamstress and made the majority of Valerie's clothing. She was very skilled and took great pride in the many compliments received about her outstanding sewing skills. In turn, Valerie loved the attention received from the school staff and everyone else. It was just about the time that she developed a keen sense of fashion, and at five years old, her appearance was already important to her, so much so that she often had to be reminded to go out for recess.

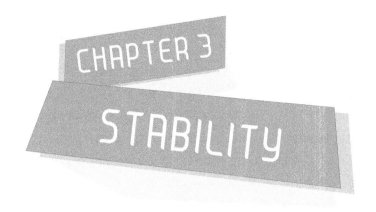

CHAPTER 3
STABILITY

V alerie's day to day life was typical as most girls her age, she went to school, did homework, played outside when she got home, watched television, and went to bed. Life went this way for her until around the age of eight when she began to notice her mom gaining weight. She would soon learn that Mary was pregnant.

In time, Mary had a son, and Valerie had a new baby brother. This was somewhat of a jolt to the now nine-year-old, Valerie, who had been the baby of the family. She was no longer the youngest of three. However, Valerie loved her new brother who was named Joshua. And she always tried helping with him in any way she could.

Just as Valerie was making the adjustment to no longer being the baby of the family, by the time he was around six months old, Joshua began having breathing problems. One night it got very bad, and the paramedics were called, unfortunately he had experienced loss of oxygen for too long and this caused severe brain damage, resulting in major disabilities.

Joshua's presence, and now his disability, brought a brand-new dynamic into the family life. And Valerie still being a child herself, was struggling to understand why this turnabout has happened. It was clear that life now revolved around Joshua—he needed 24-hour care from the family. She knew he was ill, that it was serious, and she truly loved him, but his needs came first. This dynamic was creating an inner conflict for her as it presented a vivid reminder of the questions she used to have about not having her birth mother's love—was it happening again? Was she going to be caught up on the short end of the stick again? She was both perplexed and conflicted about the transition that was happening in the household. This new baby's needs were going to come first, and that was that.

Prior to baby Joshua's birth, Valerie didn't attend church except for the standard "church days"—Easter, Christmas or special occasions. However, as a result of Joshua's illness Mary started watching Christian television and believing in God for a healing for e her baby. The family began partaking in church on a large scale. Valerie subsequently had many childhood memories of going to various healing services, and tent revivals, and eventually the family joined a local church. Valerie gave her mom credit for introducing her to Christ at a young age, and though she didn't always walk the straight and narrow, she had a great foundation. This would prove to be very important to her before all was said and done.

CHAPTER 4

LIFE CHANGES AND COPING MECHANISMS

The family's challenges were becoming all-consuming, and by the time she entered her teens during the 60's she developed a bit of a rebellious streak and could be a tad stubborn. Her parents did not spare the rod, so to speak, and this was a time when corporal punishment was acceptable and more of a societal norm. So, it was not uncommon that she may have tried to stay out late, or even talk back a bit, and she would find herself at the end of a strap.

But there was tension all around. Between the needs of Joshua, and financial pressure on her dad since Mary given up her full-time job to care for Joshua, her dad had started drinking excessively. This was very uncomfortable as it began to trigger Valerie—she never forgot that her mother pretty much chose drugs and alcohol over her. Yes, it is safe to say that the family was really going through at this point.

Watching her father head into the same direction as her birth mother and maternal grandmother was very disturbing to Valerie. She was stunned and saddened by the turn of events happening in the household that had been the stability she had been missing for most of her life. Things were really breaking down as the result of everyone having to care for a special needs child as well as three other children.

Aside from her dad's increased drinking, she found her mother to be in a bad mood most of the time. She didn't laugh and talk the way she used to, there was very little time for sewing, and she always seemed distracted and so tired all the time. Everyone seemed to be breaking under the stress. But the most drastic change of all was that she—Valerie—seemed to be the object of their stress. She was verbally abused by her parents, she actually received whippings. It was most distressing. Even though she understood that the stress from the family dynamics was the reason behind what was happening to her, still, her old feelings of being unloved overtook her again. It was a very confusing time because at the same time Valerie truly believed they were trying to do the best they could but were overwhelmed by their present situation.

Still, as she grew older, Valerie continued doing the best she could to be a respectable, God fearing daughter—the kind of daughter they could be proud of.

Mary's deeper involvement in the church after Joshua's illness, also resulted in Valerie's involvement. God had become Valerie's refuge. In other words, she had learned to lean and depend on God. She felt she really needed him now.

As she became a young woman, Valerie was grateful for her faith, it really helped her to cope during this difficult time. She was a part of the Pentecostal Church, and they were pretty ridged. Three services on any given Sunday, so many rules and guidelines they were mandated to abide by like women couldn't wear pants or make up. They didn't go to movies, listen to secular music, and so much more. These experiences impacted her memory from the time she was thirteen, and though she was not perfect, she gave God as she could. She was even teased at school because of the way she dressed, "old style and homely." But even at this young age she accepted that God's way was the way for her. God was a source of strength for her, and even if she strayed, that belief served as an additional coping mechanism for her in handling the turmoil in her home. And it really helped now with the family being in such a strained state—there were many days she dreaded going home because of the constant tension. It was not pleasant navigating in such an environment, feeling you were constantly walking on eggshells, working hard to keep peace. It was incredibly stressful, but she kept the faith and believed that life had to get better.

CHAPTER 5
CLOUDY DAYS

Valerie would reach her adolescence, and though by then she understood that her father had to make the decision to take her from her birth mom, she never could shake the feelings of abandonment from not having her mother in her life. She still questioned *"Did she not want me? And if she did, why couldn't she choose me over the drugs? Why didn't she just give them up?"*

All the questions remained, and she still wanted the answers—she needed them.

Valerie would finally get her answers. Unfortunately, it would not be until her birth mom was on her deathbed.

It was a powerful moment. She had not seen her mother in years, and when she learned of her illness, she made the decision to visit her at the hospital. Valerie was not prepared for the little shriveled up old woman lying in the bed. Even as she approached the bed, she marveled that this was NOT who she remembered her mother to be. There was still something in her mother's eyes that she recognized.

Clearly the illness and the years of drug abuse had taken a toll on her mother. When her mother focused her eyes and recognized her daughter, a tear creeped out of the corner of her eye. She raised a hand to Valerie, and in a weakened voice she spoke to her.

"Oh Valerie, baby I'm so sorry, I'm so sorry that I was never the mother you deserved to have." The tears came then, and the mother Valerie never believed loved her, sobbed and continued, "I did love you, I did, I wanted so much to be right by you, I just couldn't get past my addiction. I really loved my children, but I just couldn't fight the drugs."

As she stood and looked down at her mother, Valerie felt a wave of relief wash over her, in this instant, the sound of her mother's words pierced her heart, but in a good way. She heard with her own ears that; indeed, her mother had loved her and did want to be with her.

She gave thanks to God in that moment and at the same time said to her mother "I forgive you, Mom." They both cried before the visit ended. It was crystal clear to Valerie as never before, that her dad had made the right choice. And it also saddened Valerie when she understood that her mother absolutely did not have the capacity to raise her and her siblings not just because of her own drug and alcohol issues, but the lack of support from my mother's mom, who was dealing with her own addiction demons, too.

She was happy she got the closure she needed and now she could focus on her healing as she transitioned to becoming a young adult.

Valerie knew that as part of that healing and making progress successfully in life and to have a productive future, it would be both important and necessary to deal with her past with some type of therapy. However, for the moment, she chose to simply put a band aid on her old wounds. She just taught herself how to cover up, pretend like things were okay, and to just deal with life's challenges. She made choices that didn't always lend itself to her personal well-being. For instance, she always positioned herself to always be the peacemaker of the family.

As such she avoided conflict like the plague, sometimes she'd go so far as to take the blame for things. One time a portable radio had been broken in the house. My mom demanded to know who broke it, because she listened to her gospel music Sundays and she went on and on about this broken radio. Valerie finally just took the blame.

"Momma, I did it. It was an accident, but I did it." She knew her brothers were not going to speak up, so she took the blame. This would happen more often than not, just so there would be peace in the home. Unfortunately, over the years she lost herself in the process. She wasn't sure of her own true nature or of who she was as a woman.

She was always pretending something was okay when she wasn't or pretending to be someone she wasn't and as a result she was often stuck trying to identify her own needs. Additionally, the band aids would peel off, re-opening the issues and wounds from her past where she felt unloved and abandoned feeling unworthy or undeserving of love. Regrettably, her Pentecostal teachings fed into these misguided notions. This combination, along with the "missing" mother love as a child, blinded her and she didn't really see that her outer beauty covered up her unresolved internal conflicts. These were issues that needed attention thus making her a perfect candidate for the relationship she entered into with Mike.

It was around this time *that one* day after work, Valerie ran into an old high school friend, Sheila Williams. The two decided to get some dinner and get all caught up. Sheila, who was a few years older than Valerie, shared that her previous roommate had recently moved out and so she invited Valerie to move in with her. Valerie was very excited with this invitation and saw it as an opportunity to really spread her wings—and she accepted.

Reflections:
1. Valerie had an extremely troublesome childhood which included: abandonment, neglect, abuse, hopelessness, and even bullying. She had a lot going on and it set the stage for the weakened state her emotions were in as an adult.

2. Valerie was left with little to no self-worth or self-esteem. She considered getting professional counseling but wasn't ready. She erroneously thought leaving her childhood home was the answer.

CHAPTER 6

HONEYMOON PERIOD
MIKE AND VALERIE

Following the afternoon that Mike reached out to Valerie and they talked that night, things moved swiftly. They were then speaking on the phone on a daily basis, sometimes up to three times a day. It seemed to be love at first sight. Prior to meeting Mike, Valerie's life was pretty basic and routine. She went to work and after work she'd head over to her parents' home to run errands or help out with Joshua. Even though she'd moved out, she always made herself available for the family. Valerie always checked her messages she got home and there would be up to three messages or more from Mike. This should have been a red flag. She would call him back, and the first thing he would say was, "Hey where you been?"

"Visiting my parents . . . and how are you?"

That's how the majority of their calls began.

Valerie and Mike would talk for hours at a time as the conversations were about their childhoods, friends, family, and television. She started feeling extremely comfortable with him and she opened up to him about many private parts of her life, especially her troublesome childhood. Valerie didn't notice he wasn't as forthcoming as she was.

And she never met any of his friends. Valerie found that strange, but she didn't question it. She felt as though they were becoming best friends and she loved it. Valerie couldn't wait for her workday to end to talk to Mike. She felt on top of the world, like she was living her best life with having her own place and starting a romantic relationship. One night they were having a great conversation and a question of dating came up. He asked, "How many boyfriends or past relationships have you had?"

He wanted every detail of her past, which made her feel some anxiety. Valerie didn't want to share too much too soon. The next question literally blew her away. He asked about her first sexual experience and how it was. Though she was unprepared for this question, however, she didn't have anything to hide because she was a virgin. Still, Valerie was nervous about his reaction. The question stopped her in her tracks, and she could not imagine how he would take that news. She knew it could go either way. He could love it that he potentially could be her first or may think it is weird, or he may want someone with experience. Valerie finally got the courage to speak, "I have never had a sexual experience before—I'm a virgin."

It seemed like she was holding the phone for three minutes. There was complete silence on the other end, and it was deafening.

Valerie finally said, "Hello . . . are you still there?"

Mike finally spoke, "Did you say you were a virgin?" He simply couldn't believe it. He couldn't believe Valerie was a 27-year-old virgin. "As fine as you are, how is that possible?"

She explained to him that being raised Pentecostal and having strict parents who made sure she was sheltered enabled her to remain untouched. Additionally, she did not want to make a mistake and have a child out of wedlock. She sincerely desired to live a Godly life, therefore, it wasn't that difficult. "You don't miss what you've never had."

It seemed like after Valerie disclosed her virginity, he started becoming obsessed with her. On any given day he called up to ten times and didn't really want anything, just her whereabouts. And now, all their conversations seem to always end up talking about sex.

She was adult enough to know that ultimately, things were going to get physical between them, and it made her nervous because she had no sexual experience. At this point in their relationship, Mike was at her apartment just about every day, eating dinner together, watching videos, and a lot of kissing and heavy petting. Things were moving in the direction so that she made the decision Mike would be her first lover. It helped that she felt she was falling in love with him. Yet, it was perplexing that he was still struggling to believe it since he learned of her virginity. It was unheard of that a beautiful woman in her mid-twenties had never been with a man in his world.

They continued to enjoy each other's company. Their time consisted of sharing nightly dinner or picking up take-out. They watched lots of TV and made out a lot. The one issue she found is that they never went out on any dates and this was a problem for Valerie.

She began to bring that to his attention. "Mike, why don't we go out some time?"

He always seemed to have excuses as to why not. And again, she grew conflicted because she really loved him and was happy the way they were, but it bothered her. She no longer asked after a while, but because she was not a "homebody," she brought it up to him again, and his anger flared up for the first time.

"Mike, how about we go to a movie this weekend?"

He snapped back, "Why you keep bothering me with that . . . ain't I enough for you?"

"It has nothing to do with you being enough, Mike. I just think it would be nice. I would like us to go out sometime."

There were times when Valerie hung out with her friends. She continued to hang with them, but she saw that after being with friends after work for dinner or a drink or a sporting event, Mike had a definite attitude. Instead of bringing it up and having a conversation about it, she dismissed it. And the next time she'd have plans with friends, she'd get attitude from him again. It was becoming a real issue, and it bothered her. But Valerie continued to ignore it.

Their relationship was now into its eighth month and now it was official—they were going together. They had a good routine of getting together most days after work and getting closer and closer. She had met his parents and they adored her. So, they spent a great deal of time at their home, so much so, that she was concerned about wearing out her welcome. But the hospitality shown to her by his entire family demonstrated that they were not getting tired of her. Valerie fully embraced their kindness and the way they welcomed her with open arms was very important to her—she was feeling their love.

Her roommate, Sheila, and her boyfriend, John, also really liked Mike. Many evenings the four of them hung out, ate dinner, and sometimes played cards. This was very comforting to Valerie as well. Still there were many unsettling aspects of their relationship—things she couldn't put her finger on—and she also kept her putting off bringing Mike home to meet her parents.

First there was the subject of her virginity, Mike seemed to continue holding on to the thought that she was being untruthful. Whenever the topic came up, and it did often, he'd challenge her.

He lashed out, "How can you do it?"

She explained again, "You don't miss what you never had."

He just shook his head in disbelief. She'd end up repeating her reasons for remaining a virgin—they were her religious conviction, she didn't want children out of wedlock, and she didn't want to be a statistic.

Along with this, she still wasn't ready to introduce him to her parents. She felt strongly they would disapprove of him. It was not confirmed, but Mike was supposedly an ex-drug dealer, and he still looked the part. Her parents were locked into their religious standards and Valerie believed that he would not be welcomed by them nor held in the high regard in which his family held her.

At the same time, Mike was beginning to put pressure on her to meet them, and she knew she couldn't keep putting him off with excuses. Then, out of the blue, one night during a conversation, he randomly brought up that he had a court date coming up. Stunned at his nonchalant manner of delivery, she asked, "What is this case about?"

"I'm already paying restitution. I probably won't get any time," he responded.

Not ready for that answer, she froze and a small voice inside her head asked, "What have I gotten myself into?'

Mike told her later, "They won't show up anyway." What he meant was, she found out later, they *would disappear*, because he had them taken care of."

These revelations added to the unsettled feelings she had about the relationship and the increase desire to put off meeting her parents. And even though in her mind she knew this did not sound like a person she should be so swept away with, though her heart and her body were "all in", her gut instincts were drowned out and ignored.

Valerie nervously shared with Sheila Mike's newfound court date information.

"This sounds like a dangerous man to me, Sheila, and I am just not comfortable with it at all."

Sheila brushed it off by suggesting that perhaps he was now a "changed man."

"I had a friend who dated an ex-con once and he totally changed his life around. Valerie, I don't think you should be so hasty."

"I know, but I, uhh . . . but you know, something does not feel right about this—I'm just not sure."

"Valerie, we all have skeletons in our closet. He's really nice, don't you mess around and sabotage this relationship."

Valerie really valued her friend's opinion, so she committed to re-think this and consider that perhaps he had changed.

The next night would finally be the night that Valerie and Mike took their relationship to the next level. It started out like any other night. He came to her house for dinner. They ate, watched a movie, engaged in their usual romantic display of affection. But it did not stop there this time. Things got hotter, as they made their way to her bedroom and made love for the first time.

Whatever Valerie thought that first time would be didn't happen, and she had to admit to herself that she was disappointed. She thought she would feel a certain way, see stars, rockets taking off, something but instead it was a quick and painful act.

However, for her, far more painful than the sex act itself, was the painful words that came from Mike's mouth. "You were not a virgin, you didn't bleed!"

These words hurt to the core and that was putting it mildly. She was devastated, she felt like all of the years of saving herself were in vain, she also felt she gave away something so precious to someone who didn't believe or respect her.

All Valerie could muster up to say was, "Everyone doesn't bleed."

Valerie didn't completely get over Mike's words, but she was trying not to hold it against him, after all, he did apologize. She and Mike became closer, and their sex life began to improve as his lovemaking was slow and attentive. He made her feel so good in every aspect of the word. And though she really couldn't compare him to others, all she knew was he made her body shake and quiver after she experienced orgasm after orgasm.

She began to love him more and on a whole new level. Additionally, Valerie noticed after their relationship became physical, he became more and more obsessed with her. He began interrogating her every time she was out with friends, questioning her whereabouts, and wanting to know who she was with at all times.

She also noticed his behavior was changing, too. His jealousy was really kicking in. While they watched television one night, he saw her phone book out on the table and picked it up. He proceeded to question her about every male name he saw. Valerie was somewhat naïve of this kind controlling behavior but initially found this to be flattering.

She didn't have a clue of what the future was going to be like with him, and what's more, she was not prepared for it. His questions about the men in the book continued and each one seemed to always include a question like "Was he someone you liked for a boyfriend? or "How far did you go with him," and "Did you want to have sex with him?"

Afterward he really got fixated on one of Valerie's high school friends and it became almost unbearable; the questions were unending.

Reflection:
1. There are many things Valerie could have done differently about the relationship.

2. She could have made sure of his job status and not just accept a fake business card.

3. She could have set boundaries and not start a sexual relationship as it clouded her judgement.

4. She definitely could have asked him more questions about his past criminal activities.

5. She allowed him to control her by answering questions such as her whereabouts, etc.

6. Valerie could have insisted on meeting his friends, that would have shown her a great deal about him.

CHAPTER 5
THE GAMES BEGIN

Valerie had a great deal of mixed emotions around her relationship with Mike. While she was clear that she was in love with him, she was sometimes confused as to whether she was just caught up in the sex. She knew for sure she was hooked on that part of it. And she found herself making excuses for the behavior he continued to exhibit.

He was consuming every aspect of her life. She didn't own a car, so walking to work was part of her routine—she enjoyed it for the exercise and the money she saved on bus fare. It wasn't long after that he took that over and became her private chauffeur. On one hand it was good, but on the other hand she was beginning to feel smothered because he also picked her up from work. He began timing her visits to the family and definitely was not at all happy when she went out with friends.

At first, she thought this growing jealousy was cute and attributed it to just how much he loved her. She spent a great deal of her life feeling somewhat unloved and Mike was causing her to feel what she longed for. But more and more, the feeling began leaving her a bit uncomfortable and it started to become more of a grave concern.

Sheila and their friends started noticing a change in her, the once outgoing, vibrant, full-of-life Valerie had become distant and withdrawn as she now was canceling outings with friends and seemed to be clinging more and more to Mike.

One evening when she came home, Sheila suggested they go to the mall and get a bite to eat together.

"Come on Valerie, we haven't gotten together in a long time, let's go shopping, I need some new shoes, and then we can grab some dinner after."

"Naw, I don't think so Shelia, Mike's coming over, we'll be hanging out.

Sheila didn't like what she saw in her roommate and decided she would have a talk with her when she got back from the mall. Later that evening, she entered the apartment and called out to Valerie. She definitely wanted to be sure Mike was gone.

Valerie responded, "Hey what's up."

Sheila put her bags down, poured a glass of wine, and sat down. "Listen Valerie, I just wanted to talk to you a little about you and Mike. What's going on with you guys?"

"What do you mean, Sheila?"

"I hope you won't get mad, Valerie, but you have changed, you don't go anywhere but work, you no longer hang with your friends . . . it's just Mike . . . like . . . Valerie, every day. You're forgetting you."

Valerie was taken aback and offended by Sheila's loud declaration, but deep down inside, she knew her friend was telling the truth. She just felt torn and didn't know what to do about her situation. She loved Mike, but she knew her friend was right. And had to admit that, in spite of her feelings, this kind of attention no longer felt quite right—he was smothering her. And in this short time, they'd been together she felt herself sort of losing control.

She chose not to get into a back-and-forth exchange with Sheila, and just ended the conversation, by saying, "Well things do change once you get a regular man, and that's what I have now . . . and really Sheila, I am not interested in talking to you about this."

She turned and went off to her room.

Ten months into the relationship, and things between Valerie and Mike had slipped into a regular pattern. Every evening he pulled up at her job, literally two minutes before her quitting time. Often, she would go with Mike to his parents' house, whom she had really grown to love. She enjoyed going to their home and, while she hoped they were not getting tired of her, she loved his mom's meals. She was an excellent cook. In the meantime, Mike had still not met her parents. The closest he got was when he had dropped her off at the door many times, but she never brought him in.

She was still concerned about what they would think. They had done everything they could to protect her from certain elements in life and him being a "street" guy would not be a good fit, especially not for a "church girl" like Valerie. Even though he came from a good home, it is his "street life" she knew her parents would object to. She hadn't been able to make the introduction as yet.

In the meantime, they were getting closer, spending just about all of their time together and it felt to her like his *obsession* with her was becoming more intense. It was safe to say they were almost inseparable. One day while visiting his parents' house, Mike asked her, "When am I going to meet your parents?"

Soon it no longer could be avoided.

One Friday night he put his foot down and said, "I'm coming in tonight to meet your parents" when I pick you up. Valerie felt a prickle of fear, but she reluctantly said, "Okay."

That night she paced back and forth like an expectant father, waiting for him to arrive. Even though she was certainly of age and had been on her own for a while now, she still worried about what her parents thought about her, and the decisions she made.

Soon, there was a knock at her parents' door around the same time her dad arrived home from work.

It was him.

Valerie let Mike in, who looked really nice, but her main concern was did he drive his *pimped out*, luxury car, the one that screamed *dope dealer*. She peered out the peephole and sure enough—he had.

He came in and sat on the sofa. Her mom hadn't cooked so she went to get some take-out. After Valerie's mom returned with the dinner, they say, and ate. Things seemed to be progressing well as he got along very well and actually appeared to be enjoying himself.

Mike seemed to fit right in and made himself at home. Her parents were gracious and conversational at best. It was getting late as Valerie could tell her parents were getting tired, so she called it a night. Mike thanked her parents for their hospitality, and they said goodbye and left. Valerie was hopeful that her parents liked and accepted him. She would find out quicker than even she thought.

She loved the opportunity that Saturday mornings brought to sleep in. Her Saturday morning sleep in was disrupted by the phone call she dreaded. It was Mary.

"Good morning, Mom, how are you?"

"I'm fine. Listen I want to ask you, where did you meet that guy?"

"Who, mom?"

"You know who I'm talking about . . . don't pretend with me, your boyfriend, that's who," she snapped sharply.

"Here it is, Valerie, he can't come back here. I don't know where you found him, but you need to let him get back there. He can't come to this house again."

"Mom, what? Why . . . are you acting like this?'

"We didn't raise you to take up with no guy like that. He looks like some kind of pimp or something. Don't ask me why, he just can't come here and that's final You are grown now, you can do what you want, but we don't have to approve. Does he even go to church? Looks like you totally gave up the church anyway since you been with him. Well, me and your daddy, we ain't going support that behavior and you running around with that guy."

While she knew her parents might have some struggles with her relationship, she wasn't ready for the tirade she received that morning from her mom. She knew they were disappointed that her church attendance had decreased, and that it appeared to them that she had turned her back on her upbringing. Despite the occasional Sunday service appearance or two, she truly missed the church engagements, and missed the close relationship she used to have with the Lord. Indeed, she was conflicted, and in spite of it all, her feelings for Mike seemed to grow. And now her parents have told her he is not welcomed in their home again.

What she dreaded the most, knowing his sensitivity, and having seen small examples of his capacity for anger, was how to tell him of her parent's decision.

Over the next week or two, Mike didn't mention anything about her parents. She was glad but knew his feelings were going to be hurt, and she knew they needed to have a conversation. Their routine continued and in the ensuing days, as usual, he picks her up from work and they go to his parents' place. Eventually they'd make it to her apartment, watch a little television, talk about their day, and of course have sex. This continued and her passion for him continued to increase.

This is why when he asked when they were going back to visit her parents, as difficult as it was, she had to just come right out and tell him.

On the sofa one evening she had the conversation with him. "Mike, I'm sorry my parents have said I should not bring you back over."

He was blindsided by what she told him.

"What . . . ," he said, "What do you mean?"

"Just that, Mike, my parents are strict, and my mom is a devout, born again Christian and they see you in direct conflict of the way I was raised. I'm sorry, I hate it, but that is just the way it is."

"Damn, what have I done? They don't know nothing about me. I been a lot of things, but I ain't never been banned from anyone's home before."

Mike was almost shouting now.

Valerie didn't know what else to say as she couldn't say anything to make him understand. She just hung her head and prayed for this moment to be over.

Over the next time period, as they continued as they had been, there was blessedly no further mention of her parents or their decision. Valerie continued to ponder over a few things about her current status with Mike. First was the matter of her church and how falling back from it was impacting her—it bothered her mentally that she was no longer in regular attendance. She deeply regretted feeling more separated from God, but what could she expect when she only attended mostly when prompted by her mom, and other than that it was only when she felt like it.

Inside, she knew the reason for this, it was difficult for her to sit up in church whose tenets were all a part of her upbringing—the do's and don'ts—listening to sermons, when she herself was regularly engaging in pre-marital sex. The hypocrite in her spoke loudly within.

The other troubling place for her was how she had completely become separated from her friends. She really did love Mike, but she did not see why he struggled so hard with her maintaining her friendships—well she could maintain the friendships, she just couldn't hang out with them without Mike's negative response. She couldn't think of the last time she hung out with them. She and Mike were literally together all of the time. When her friends would reach out, she always made an excuse for the disconnect.

This was deeply troublesome to her, because she enjoyed being with her friends and missed them a lot. But whenever she did, he gave her the silent treatment when she returned, or gave her attitude, but mostly made negative comments about them. But by avoiding them altogether, she attempted to dismiss this as manipulation and control, yet it was the yang to the yin of Mike. And it left her feeling uneasy at best.

It had been weeks now, and Mike still had not made any further response about her parents, part of her was glad, but she still would have like to know what he was thinking. This is where some of her uneasiness occurred. And it didn't help that he was slipping more and more deeply to his obsessiveness around his imagined thoughts about guys from her past—of which truly there was nothing of significance, she reminds him constantly she had been a virgin when they got together.

One weekend she was supposed to go to church with family, but that changed when in an unusual move. He had come over early that Sunday morning and they had breakfast together. Sheila and her boyfriend, John, were also a part of the impromptu meal with them too, though, they had a great time.

But the pleasantries were short lived when *that* evening things switched up revealing how stuck he was on her "non-existent past." The jealousy brought on by his senseless insecurity just randomly came up once again. And while at this point in the relationship she had gotten accustomed to it this time it was different.

Out of the blue, Mike asked her about one of the young men he saw in her phone book several months prior. He started again with the questions,

"Are you still attracted to him? Do you still talk to him?"

Valerie reassured him he was enough for her, and she was happy with just him. But the questions continued and spilled over to her whereabouts, and who she was going with and when and where they were to return along with this insistence of taking her and picking her up from everywhere.

His jealousy was becoming exhausting. The obsession and constant disbelief were becoming maddening. One day he called her and let her know he couldn't pick her up from work. This change made her happy to walk home. It had been a while since she felt the wind and the sun against her skin on those walks. However, a young man approached her and asked for her number. She told him she had a boyfriend and continued to walk away from him. The encounter with him didn't sit well with her as she felt like a set-up.

She was right as later on that night while eating dinner, the conversation came up that would lead to a most bizarre episode.

"Well, you passed the test."

"What do you mean, Mike?"

"That guy who came up to you today and asked you for your number.

She looked at him incredulously. "Yes, what about him?"

He laughed then said, "Uh . . . that was not a chance encounter."

This disturbed Valerie in a major way. She wanted to let him know how disturbing this was, but his demeanor soon changed. He became very anxious and started in about his fear of being cheated on.

"I always get cheated on. I'm always getting hurt." Then in a very threatening tone said, "You better not hurt me like the rest of them."

She assured him over and over that she loved him and would never hurt him. She concluded by telling him, "I am faithful to you."

This was becoming too much for her as it was draining. She didn't know what else to do to prove herself to him. Then in the next instant, right before eyes, Mike began to cry. At first, she thought it was a joke, but she noticed his sobs were genuine as he seemed to now be an inconsolable man.

He cried some more for about an hour straight as it unnerved her to see him like this. They were out in the living room before she finally ushered him into her bedroom. The last thing she wanted was for Sheila and John to come into the apartment to see him like that for it was embarrassing. He cried some more until he finally got himself together and left to go home. She watched him walk away from her apartment to his car. She felt somewhat responsible for his sadness and she allowed him to manipulate her again. On some level she knew and felt relieved and however she knew the relationship was over. She knew she would miss him but, she was deeply concerned about his well-because she really loved him.

Reflections:

1. There were so many red flags in this chapter that Valerie overlooked.

2. Valerie could have set boundaries or ended the relationship.

3. The mind games were endless, setting her up to prove her faithfulness?

4. The constant jealousy rants, his insecurities were a form of control. And signs that he was unstable.

5. Mike becoming her personal chauffeur, utilizing control tactics, and sabotaging her friendships, plus always wanting to her whereabouts—were parts of establishing control over her entire life.

CHAPTER 8

PHYSICAL ABUSE BEGINS

Valerie went to work the following day with constant flashbacks from last night. She couldn't shake wondering what his state of mind was and she was convinced he had mental issues. She planned on check on him when she got home. She had to admit it was nice not being picked up, and she definitely didn't mind the walk home. Valerie was being so smothered lately by him she welcomed being alone. She got home, changed her clothes to comfortable clothes, and enjoyed television alone before Sheila arrived.

As she reached for the phone, it rang.

It was him.

The first thing Valerie asked was he alright.

"I'm fine . . . what are you doing?"

She told him she had just gotten home. They talked about fifteen minutes before he asked to come over. Valerie was surprised because she really thought their relationship was over after his emotional rants and accusations the night before. The creepy thing about it was, he was acted as though nothing happened the night before and this disturbed her.

Mike literally ignored what happened the night before, and it was clear he expected her to do the same. But that wasn't about to happen as the memories of his emotional breakdown would forever be etched in her mind. She was totally confused and somewhat disappointed. She was really tired of his jealousy, suspicions, and psychotic behavior. Against her better judgement, Valerie allowed him to come over. They talked about everything *but* his erratic behavior from last night. She figured he was embarrassed that she saw him like that. Sure enough, they talked more, then ate, and had the best sex ever.

He was more attentive to her than ever before as they made passionate love for hours. She figured this is what "make-up sex" was all about. Valerie was not proud of allowing him to draw her back in. But still something was different for Valerie now. Her mind rehashed the jealousy and all-too-familiar control tactics. But she wasn't able to shake the last episode. The image of him shaking and sobbing and going on and on about her cheating on him was right behind her eyelids.

The next day Mike picked her up from work, back to the same routine, but instead of going to visit his parents, they went straight to Valerie's apartment.

Mike said, "My mom finished the movie you've been waiting to see . . . let's watch it before Sheila gets home."

Valerie nodded, he put the movie in the VCR, and they began to watch it. The movie was in for about twenty minutes before her phone went off and interrupted them. She went into her bedroom to answer the phone. It was her mother. She was calling with to say that Valerie's high school classmate, ironically the one Mike obsessed over when looking in her phone book, said for her to call him. Valerie had no intentions of calling him back, so she didn't even write the number down her mom stated.

Valerie went back into the living room, sat down next to Mike, in hopes of being uninterrupted. She got comfortable on the couch next to Mike and seconds later, her life would never be the same.

Mike asked, "Who was on the phone?"

"My mom."

"What did she want?"

His questions were not a surprise as she had gotten used to his interrogations, but what was strange was him being so concerned about what her mom wanted. All of a sudden, the weirdest feeling consumed her.

As she thought about his behavior of late and the episode from the night before and everything he demonstrated, she felt the urge to run. She sensed that she was in danger.

And then it happened.

He snapped, got enraged and yelled, "Who was that on the phone?"

She was shocked.

"Mike, I told you . . . it was my mom. She gave me a message that an old classmate had called me."

He screamed at her, "Go get that number you wrote down."

Valerie now knew her life was in jeopardy. She looked for a quick exit out her front door as Mike looked like pure evil. He towered over her in height and was just about one hundred pounds heavier than her. She knew he would catch her, and she didn't know if his gun was on him as she knew he had them in his car.

She stood up to run but her legs wobbled like Jell-o. She had never been so scared in her life—it was so surreal. She mustered the strength and courage to move. He followed close behind her. She didn't know what was going on as he had never treated her this way. It was like a nightmare and it was happening to her. As he was on her heels walking close behind her, she realized he set her up, just like he had hired the guy who approached her for her phone number the other day.

He continued to yell, "Where is it?"

She confessed she never wrote it down.

He shouted to told her that this was indeed another set up.

"Yeah, I knew you was go' n lie . . . I had my boy call your mom and pretend to be your classmate and left his phone number. Why did you lie to me? You didn't tell me that guy called you, you made it seem like it was a co-worker. All you had to do was tell me the truth. You are just like the other women, you lied and hurt me."

The next sequence of events shocked her as he took his hand and slapped her across the face with all of his might. Her face stung so bad because she had never been hit so hard. She tried to run, but by this time, he grabbed her by the neck, and threw her onto the bed, closed his fist, and punched every inch of her body.

He beat her unmercifully as he continued to punch her in the face, her head, stomach, everywhere. His slaps were the most excruciating, with each stinging tear rolling down her face. She continued to apologize so that he would stop, but it seemed like the tears energized him the more. The beating went on so long Valerie wasn't sure if it was pure exhaustion, she was feeling or if she was going in and out of consciousness.

He kept beating her until Sheila came home. She heard the ruckus coming from Valerie's room, but the locked door stopped her attempts to barge in. He stopped momentarily and threatened to kill both of them if they said anything.

"I know where Sheila works, and where her parents live and yours as well and all I have to do is call my homeboy . . . and none of you will see the sun again."

She complied because she was terrified because she knew he had high powered weaponry to back his claims.

Sheila said through the door, "Hey . . . girl how's it going?"

"I'm fine," Valerie said through her busted lip.

She cleared her throat so Sheila couldn't tell she was crying. She didn't want to involve her roommate.

Sheila continued, "Girl I'm headed out."

Reluctantly, Valerie said, "Okay."

Sheila could sense something was wrong. "Girl let me see you, you might look different."

Valerie wanted to scream help me, but she knew he would have shot her and her roommate. She kept the door closed and said, "Girl I'm not dressed, I'll see you when you come back."

When Sheila left, he continued to beat Valerie, and threatened her if she fell asleep, he was going to shoot her. He beat her so bad that her body ached with throbs of pain that pulsated frequently it prevented her to move. Every inch of her body was in pain. She also tasted a salty familiar substance—her own blood. She knew he busted her lip. She was well aware the inevitable was coming soon. Valerie repented to the Lord as her life flashed before her. She saw her parents, siblings, even her dreams of motherhood.

Everyone she loved flashed before her. She was so weak she couldn't keep her eyes open, at some point he stopped beating her and she drifted off to sleep. She remembered he woke her up, at about 2:00am, to say he was headed home. He continued to threaten her that if she called the police or told anyone he would send his homeboys to take care of her family. Valerie believed him as he already had people following her and she knew he had weapons.

After she closed the door behind him, she went into the bathroom to see how bad she looked. She was afraid to look as he showed no mercy for her. She wasn't worried about Sheila seeing her because she had already left for work. She turned the light on, looked in the mirror, and was horrified at what she saw. She sobbed uncontrollably, not because of the pain but she was unrecognizable. Her face was swollen about three times its normal size and she had two black eyes. Her nose and lips were swollen, blood and feces were on her clothes as he had raped and sodomized her in between the beatings.

Valerie could hardly walk from room to room as her body was so sore. As she stumbled around, her phone rang—it was her mom. She never called that early on a weekday and she was hoped nothing was wrong. She answered hello and the first thing that came out of her mom's mouth was she okay? Valerie was so confused as she wondered did her mom know. Did he do something to her parents? Her mom said her car had been vandalized in her driveway. Valerie froze and didn't know what to say to her mom. She was terrified to tell her what had happened. Could he had something to do with the vandalizing of her mom's car? What else was he capable of?

Her mom assured her she was fine and hung up.

She made up in her mind no one could see her like this. If she called the police and have him arrested, he could harm or kill her and her family. Valerie immediately called her job and took some time off. There's no way she could go to work, so she made up a story that she had an illness and her doctor told her to take some time off. She had to think quickly on how she would handle this, so she decided to check herself into a hotel room and hide until her wounds healed.

Valerie grabbed some things and threw them into a suitcase and left. She then called Sheila and her mom and gave the same excuse she gave her job.

She went to the refrigerator and made sure she had enough food and whatever else she would need before she went to her hotel room because she knew if she were seen, a total stranger would call the police and she couldn't afford that. She believed Mike would harm her family and friends if she went to the police. She covered up her bruises as much as possible by wearing a really large floppy hat that covered the majority of her face and she wore dark sunglasses.

The majority of her bruises had faded away in about two weeks, the few remaining ones had to be covered up with makeup. Valerie knew she had to come out of hiding and get back to work soon. A few of her co-workers were surprised to see her wearing makeup because she never wore it before. They suspected something was up as she got second glances and whispers when she entered a room.

Sheila questioned her for leaving so abruptly and her mom also asked if she was okay. Valerie knew people weren't buying her story of a mysterious illness, they wanted to know why she disappeared for such a long time.

About two weeks after the beating, Mike reached out to Valerie and asked how she was and did she call the police on him. She assured him she didn't call them, and she wouldn't. He began blaming her for his actions or assault.

"You should have been honest with me and it wouldn't have happened."

Valerie couldn't believe the gall of him. The audacity to blame her then turning in a token apology as he thoroughly promised it would never happen again.

She felt a number of emotions all at once—anger, hurt, betrayal, but especially fear. She had never witnessed anything like this before. She pondered how she got here.

Mike slowly turned on the charm while they conversed. He let her know he still loved her and wanted to make their relationship work. Valerie knew right then and there she needed some serious counseling. Why was she even considering taking him back?

Against her better judgement she forgave Mike and moved forward with their relationship. Valerie tried pretending the beating never happened, but she found herself walking on eggshells around him and basically pretended to be a perfect girlfriend. Mike was showering her with gifts, flowers, dinners, and plenty of makeup sex. Valerie convinced herself that he would never do it again. From that day he didn't show any signs of jealousy or control tactics, she figured they were headed in the right direction.

Shortly after the beating episode, Valerie's dad came to visit her which was a rare occasion. She was concerned that something must have happened to her mom or her siblings. Her dad assured her that everyone was fine and that he came to talk to her. He began telling her that a co-worker of his saw her riding in a car with Mike and they told him whatever you do get your daughter away from him he's crazy.

Her dad's co-worker also informed him that Mike beat a relative of theirs so bad that the woman was disfigured for life, he heated up a hot iron and laid it across her face and tortured her several times. He also told her dad that he's bad news, he has several aliases, witnesses to crimes he committed have literally disappeared off the face of the earth. He surmised that he may have not killed them, but he gets the job done. Her dad informed her that Mike was extremely dangerous. "Do whatever you can to get her away from him, I hate to say it, he might kill her if you don't," the man said to my dad. Valerie wanted to reach out to her dad and tell him she believed him because of what happened to her two months prior, but she didn't disclose anything for fear of her family members becoming missing. Her dad went on to say, "I'm glad we have all of your insurance policies paid up, because you're not going to be here long, that guy is going to kill you."

The information her dad gave her solidified her fears even more, she felt trapped with a killer and didn't know how to escape. Valerie also knew by the way he had people set her up, he had people willing and ready to do violent acts for him. To make matters worse, Valerie learned that he was a notorious killer.

Valerie's father left her with this. "If you don't get away from that monster, you know he's going to kill you, don't you?"

Valerie couldn't say a word, but she knew her dad was right. After a month or so of her dad's visit, she and Mike were dating again but she never forgot her dad's warnings despite her fear of Mike. Valerie also knew she had to have an escape plan of safety for all involved.

Mike had planned a date night for them to go to a drive-in movie. He arrived at her place and appeared to be very agitated, again her instincts kicked in and she felt something was going on with him though she just didn't know what was up.

"I lost over five thousand dollars and I can't find it," he said.

That was a puzzle, because she knew one thing for certain, he didn't earn the money honestly. They had been riding for about twenty minutes heading to the movies when he turned down a familiar street. At first, she couldn't remember who lived there, then it hit her—the street of her high school friend. It was the one Mike seemed obsessed with from her phone book.

She looked over at the house, and then all hell broke loose. Mike again lost it. He yelled, "Why are you looking at your ex's house? Why are you disrespecting me?"

Before Valerie knew it, he slapped her hard across the face. Fear gripped her and all she could think of was if he had the gun. Terrified, she glanced under his car seat and saw a shining object—the gun. She was waiting for him to make a U-turn and go back to her place to finish what he started, but when he didn't, she was relieved. She sat back in her seat and prayed they were headed to the movies.

No such luck.

Mike drove a few blocks, but he wasn't headed towards the movies, or her apartment.

"What was going on . . . and where were they headed?"

He drove a couple of blocks down and pulled over, her heart raced, and it felt like it was literally going to jump out of her chest. Mike turned the car off as Valerie's palms were sweaty. She couldn't control the hard-pumping sounds in her chest that pulsated with every breath she took.

Mike looked at her in the most calm but nasty way and said, "Give me your ID and your shoes."

"What?"

He repeated. "Give me your ID and your shoes I said."

This time she knew he meant business, he then reached under his seat, and her heart sank, and her stomach flipped over. She felt absolutely nauseated like in two seconds she was going to throw up. She was certain he would kill her tonight and probably throw her in a dark ditch or something. She began to cry and pleaded for her life. At this point he had the gun in his hand and he had it pointed downward. She then reached in her purse and took out her ID and along with her shoes, handed them over.

She begins to think of a possible plan of escape. But they were in a dark and secluded place, so it didn't seem likely that she could get away. Valerie wondered how far she could run, and where could she run to, there was no civilization in sight. She felt like this was not the first time he'd done this.

Mike got out of the car walked around to her side and yelled, "Get out." He was angrier and there was more rage in his voice as he motioned her along. She saw him put something in his pocket. He then pointed it towards her and said, "Get in the trunk."

She began to shake uncontrollably as she pleaded and begged him for mercy.

"GET IN."

Valerie got in, and he closed the trunk. Even though she could not see where she was, she paid close attention to the sounds she heard. She heard the car engine, other cars passing by, but then dead silence.

Valerie stopped her tears and went into survival mode. She knew her first move should be to pray. So, she prayed and asked God again to help her get out of this alive. She didn't know how He was going to do it, but she believed He could do it. Valerie noticed the mechanism in the trunk like, among other things, the white light bulb. It felt like they were driving for hours but she knew it was probably about ten or fifteen minutes. Valerie wasn't hearing any other cars now, she figured he found a more secluded area to dump her body after he killed her. Suddenly the car stopped, and her tears returned. She feared the worse was about to happen.

She waited for the trunk to open but instead she heard him talking to someone, it sounds like a female voice, she was now really confused and wondered if this lady was his accomplice with her murder?

Valerie listened intently, desperately wondering what were they saying? It wasn't clear until she heard the woman say, "No, No don't do that, you don't want to do that!"

That was the end of their conversation.

The next thing she heard was the car door opening and Mike getting back in. He drove around for about another ten to fifteen minutes until the car stopped. She knew he was coming for her.

He got out and she heard his keys jingling.

What happened next was bizarre as he unlocked the trunk and helped her out. She was near civilization. She could see a supermarket down the street.

He yelled, "Hurry up and get out before someone sees you," as he helped her out from the trunk and brushed her clothes off. He helped her to the front seat and acted as if nothing had ever happened. Valerie said a prayer, "Lord thank you for whoever that woman was that told him not to kill me."

But she also knew that if she did not come up with a plan to get away from him, sooner or later Mike might succeed. A plan would be a challenge because she was deeply concerned about keeping her family safe. At this point, it was more than just being about her. By entering into this relationship, she had put the lives of everyone who knew her in jeopardy,

Reflection:

1. Mike's emotional instability was on full display in this chapter.

2. Valerie had a clear way out on the night of Mike's mental breakdown.

3. Valerie needed to pay closer attention to his mind games and how that was a control tactic.

4. She could have confided more to her roommate Sheila.

5. Valerie was alone because she isolated herself from everyone, his manipulation worked.

CHAPTER 9

ON AGAIN, OFF AGAIN

The three months following the ride she took in the trunk of Mike's care were deceptively great for Valerie, there were no beatings, threats, or mind games. She wondered was the worst over. She honestly didn't know but was taking it one day at a time.

Valerie was beginning to feel happiness and marriage had become a common topic of their conversations lately. Though, she did ask herself if marriage was the way to go with Mike.

Her parents were mortified when she mentioned she was considering marrying him, but at the same time they knew their hands were tied since she was an adult. On the other hand, Mike's parents were ecstatic when they heard of the possibility of wedding bells because they had really grown to love Valerie and wanted her to marry their son.

They weren't ready to get married anytime soon so they did the next best thing which was to move in together. Valerie knew her parents wouldn't approve of this either they did not believe in "living together" in the first place, least of all seeing her move in with him was a hard pill to swallow. Mike and Valerie moved into their own place about a month later, and for a while everything seemed wonderful. And though she did feel bad because she left her roommate hanging, her mindset was love conquers and she wanted to be with her man.

The first two months of living together was awesome. Valerie loved their new and exquisite place as it looked like something out of a home magazine. She had never lived in such a beautifully decorated house before. Their hangout place immediately changed, instead of being at his parents' house every day, they came to their new place. She loved coming home snuggling on the couch and making love to her man. She was really looking forward to a great future with Mike.

After those two months, it would be just a matter of weeks later that her world would come crashing down. He had been rather quiet for the last few days, she knew something was up but again, couldn't put her finger on it.

One morning she had overslept a bit and was running late for work. She dashed into the bathroom. However, she came out of the bathroom to find pictures off the wall and his things sprawled out onto the floor, bed, and everywhere else.

"Are you rearranging the furniture again?"

It wasn't uncommon for him to be moving furniture around, but this felt different.

She asked again, "Are you rearranging the furniture?"

He said, "No I'm leaving you. I can't do this."

"What are you talking about? We just moved in here two months ago."

He said, "I know it's me, I'm just not ready for a relationship like I thought I was."

She was speechless, thinking this was joke, but soon realized he was dead serious as he began to take pictures off the wall. She didn't know what to do, she really loved him. Valerie believed they were in a good place now and she didn't really want to go backwards and have to move back in with her parents. Luckily, she had a lot of sick time, so she called off from work to clear her mind and worked through some important decisions. And even though a part of her was just a tiny bit excited about what it could mean for her if he did leave, she ended up begging him not to go.

At first, he ignored her and continued to pack. He then went from ignoring her to speaking calmly then to blaming her for his decision to leave. He became irate and screamed at her several times, and out of nowhere told her to take off her clothes, she was thinking *I'm definitely not in the mood for lovemaking right now.*

Little did Valerie know she would be pleading for her life once again as he then reached under their bed, pulled out his shot gun, and aimed it at her.

He said, "How much do you love me? Are you sure you are going to stay faithful to me?"

She stood there, butt-naked, and pleaded for her life. She was crying uncontrollably again trying to run around him. She didn't care that she was naked. She was headed towards the front door. He then grabbed her, put the gun down, and spoke.

"You can go put your clothes back on. I just needed to see how much you love me!"

In that instant, she knew she had to get away from him. He was a ticking time bomb waiting to detonate. She put her clothes back on but still didn't know what his next move would be. He began putting his clothes back in the drawer, closets, and re-hung the pictures. He hadn't planned on going anywhere, it was another mind game to test her love and loyalty.

At this point she finally came to the conclusion that he was crazy. After she got showered and dressed, he was the nicest, sweetest person around. She called it "Dr. Jekyll and Mr. Hyde syndrome." She finally saw things weren't getting any better but worse.

Valerie continued to go about her daily routine of going to work then visiting his or her parents and whatnot. She was seriously planning a way of escape as she began to increase her prayer life and trusted that God would help her to get out of this abusive relationship. She told God she would serve him the rest of her life. More of Valerie's family and friends started noticing many changes in her, the once silly, playful girl who loved making everyone laugh, had become withdrawn and reserved. She was no longer the friend who loved going place and being out but morphed into a homebody.

One afternoon while visiting her parents, her mom asked, "What's wrong with you? You haven't been yourself at all lately ... what's going on?"

Valerie's initial response was somewhat nonchalant as she said, "Nothing's wrong ... I'm fine."

She then went on to make excuses about being tired and busy but her mom wasn't buying.

Valerie wanted to hug her mom and hold her like she was a little girl and assure her that everything was going to be alright. She knew if she shared anything regarding her abusive boyfriend with her mom, she would have to keep it to herself, because any information she let leak out could compromise everyone's safety.

Valerie couldn't hold the truth from her mom any longer as she confided in her and confirmed her dad was right about Mike and his violent nature, and his background of being an abuser. She later shared with her mom that he was a known killer, and many people that were to testify against him that never made it to court.

Mary listened intently to what her daughter shared. She took it seriously and told her she was praying and suggested that she should also. Her mother assured her that she believed God was going to get her out of this abusive relationship. Mary said she had sensed something bad was going on. She reiterated that she never felt good about him since her initial encounter, which is why she banned him from her home in the first place. One thing Valerie knew and loved and respected about her mom was she could get a prayer through. She also believed with her mom's prayers, that God was going to give her a way of escape.

Over the next few months, Valerie didn't experience any physical abuse, but his controlling ways were getting the best of her. She was feeling so smothered, that it was made her despise him. There was an occasion when she made the right decision not to page him. She thought *I'm a grown woman. I work.* As a matter of fact, she often worked a part-time job as well as her day job. Valerie prided herself on her great work ethic.

One particular Saturday, she rode to the part-time job with a co-worker, and the two of them decided to go to the mall after work and grab a bite to eat. Mike expected, no demanded that when she wasn't in his eyesight, that she page him and let him know her whereabouts. Valerie hated to report to him, so this time she didn't. She and her co-worker had a great time shopping and going to eat as she enjoyed the time away from him.

She didn't page him or anything and it felt good even though she knew there would be consequences. Sure enough, when she arrived home, Mike was all over her giving her the third degree about her whereabouts and yelling at her, demanding to know why she had not paged him. This went on until bedtime. Valerie was certain more than ever that she was tired of the life she was living with Mike.

In the early morning hours following the incident when she didn't page him like she was instructed to, he woke her up out of her sleep and asked her continuously why she didn't page him. She repeatedly said she forgot, and it wouldn't happen again.

Before she knew it, he threw her on the bed. She agonized over what was coming next. Mike had that same psychotic look in his eyes he had the night he first beat her, and she knew it was on. He then pushed her again on the bed this time with more force and once again she pleaded for her life. Mike unzipped his pants and threw her on her stomach and began sodomizing her. She lay there, sobbing, as he continued to violate her until his anger subsided and he did his deed. He then kicked her with his foot on her back as if she were an animal and said, "Do what I tell you."

Valerie knew for a fact she had to leave him before he killed her.

In the meantime, Valerie's mother continued to notice the decline in her daughter's demeanor without even a real clue of the hell she was experiencing in this abusive and tormenting relationship. And each passing day became harder and harder for Valerie. Again, Mike had not been physically abusive to her for several months, but the emotional abuse and mind games were taking their toll on her.

From day to day she walked on eggshells, tried to be perfect for him, never sure what would set him off. The most difficult part of it all was pretending to the world that everything was okay. She went through the motions of her life, work, visiting her parents or his parents. By now there was pretty much no contact with her friends. After the incident when she didn't page him, that was the last time she did anything with her friends He achieved what he wanted, and she didn't want to rock the boat.

Her life had become so mundane. Her friends noticed the difference in her demeanor as she wanted to scream to the mountain tops of what she was going through but, she only trusted her mom. However, she had one friend, Staci, who was more vocal than anyone else. Staci came right out and asked many times if Mike was abusing her. When Valerie said she was not being abused, Staci didn't believe her. Having been in a couple abusive relationships herself, Staci knew the signs, and she warned Valerie that she needed to leave him before it was too late. She definitely knew Staci was right, but she had to plan it out, she had her family to think of. Nonetheless, Staci knew he was abusing Valerie as the signs were all there. The rush to call or page him and every time she talked to him, she could hear the fear and anxiety in her voice. She had lived the same life many years ago and she understood what was going on.

All Valerie could remember was her dad's warnings, of what Mike previously did to his co-worker's daughter. Valerie knew if he didn't do it, he would have it done. On the other hand, she could not shake her fear for her loved ones. She couldn't risk their lives because they were innocent in this.

She found herself talking to God more and more about her situation and seeking his help in escaping from this abuser. She began to feel as if her days were numbered, it was only a matter of time before Mike would try and kill her. Valerie remembered one morning a church member of hers called her out of the blue and said, "I know you're surprised to be hearing from me. God had you on my mind. God wants you to know that He loves you, and He's going to get you out of the situation you're in."

Valerie may have been labeled a "back slider", but she was still a believer and knew God had to have shown this lady what she was going through. She was a little skeptical, but she thought about it and the only person she shared her situation with was her mom. Valerie knew her mom wasn't close enough to this individual to share such private information and she was now convinced God was on her side.

As time passed, Valerie continued to have extreme feelings of loneliness, even though she was constantly around people, but she couldn't share with anyone what she was going through. She feared

Mike so much and she knew exposing him would be detrimental to all involved. During the next couple months, the emotional pain she experienced was excruciating. She was living a complete lie. Smiling on the outside pretending everything was okay but dealing with total gloom and torment on the inside. She felt so powerless to say the least, her friends had become few in number mainly because of his control tactics. Sadly enough, Valerie still had love for him, but feared him at the same time.

He even started controlling her finances. And being with him wasn't all the financial break it was at first. Once they got their own place, it was she who was paying the rent. Oh yes, he *somehow* paid for them to get into their own place, but after that, it was all on her. The life she was living was now draining her and all she had to show for it was sex and companionship when things were going well.

She began to question herself and really exam what she was doing. Life shouldn't be this way. She even told herself she deserves better. She kept praying, and seriously talking with God about this relationship. She said, "Lord is there a way out of this? Can I get out alive, and at the same time protect my loved ones? Lord, I know if there is a way out of this, you can provide it Lord—I pray you help me."

More and more Valerie definitely feared for her life. Mike was a ticking time bomb, and she truly felt it was just a matter of time before she became a statistic—Mike would kill her.

Reflection

1. Looking back, Mike's behavior was always questionable from the beginning.

2. Mike's insecurities and jealousy had nothing to do with her.

3. Valerie allowed Mike to take away her dignity, self-worth and self-esteem.

4. Valerie allowed Mike to take her family, friends, and any outside connections away.

5. Valerie did have support and insight from Staci, she gone through similar experiences; that's why Valerie could not fool her.

CHAPTER 10

VICTORY

As Valerie began to grow more and more weary of Mike's erratic behavior, and of never knowing from one moment to the next what would send him over the top, she knew she had to make a decision for her life. Even though Valerie believed she still loved him, she could not cope with the fear.

Consequently, she began to get intentional about a plan to get out. As she increased her prayer life, her faith had also increased. Both she and her mother prayed every day, in-person and or on the phone. She began putting the pieces of her relationship with God back together again. This included talking with Him about everything she had been through. She repented for the sexual sin she had been engaging with Mike. And she included fasting in her weekly ritual to get reacquainted with God. After a time, she had begun to feel she was resuming some of her former closeness with Him.

Next and most importantly, Valerie began to accept the fact that indeed she was in an abusive relationship. And yet with her revitalized faith and the ramped-up prayer life, she wasn't seeing any results. But still she stayed committed to her belief that God had not forsaken her.

She knew she had to focus on a strategic plan to break out of this prison she was in. She knew that any wrong decisions could cost her life, or the lives of her family and friends.

Valerie also began learning about the cycle of abuse and she learned that the most dangerous time of an abusive relationship was when the victim made up their mind to leave. (*The Clarion Ledger January 28, 2017); Mitchell, Jerry.* And that the greatest violence often follows the departure. She knew a well-thought-out plan was absolutely necessary if she was to get away alive. She struggled with where to begin.

While she pondered what to do, she and Mike were doing the same things, the same old routine. Over a few weeks, things were relatively the same. However, once again, Valerie's instincts were kicking in. She sensed that something was going on with him. Their routine was not altered, going to work, visiting parents, back home watching television. But out of the blue, Mike was not talking to her. He literally hadn't talked or uttered a word to her for about seven days.

At the beginning of the "silent treatment week" as she called it, she wouldn't even know if he was taking her to work or if he was, so she walked. He did take her, but the silence was very chilling. The ride from their place to her office was the most unnerving she had ever felt. Something in her gut told her something bad was going to happen. Subsequently she began to feel like she should get away from him and quick. She knew that if an episode was coming, this time may be the one that ends her life for sure this time for sure. The following day after work Valerie had a hair appointment. Mike picked her up from work as usual but, the silence continued. It was such a relief to get her hair done and she could spend time with her hairdresser/friend that was someone other than Mike, and she wouldn't get the third degree about her whereabouts.

He was on time to pick her up from the salon and like clockwork, the unsettling feeling came back to her. Valerie wondered "what had she done" this time to make him so angry with her? When they arrived home, he initiated sex with. It had been over a week, which in and of itself was weird, because he never made it past three days without sex. His body language showed he wanted sex as he began to kiss her and proceeded to undress her, all the while he stayed silent. Valerie took a shower afterwards to wash off his residue. He seemed to enjoy the act far more than she cared for it. It was hard to get into lovemaking with dead silence. She had creepy feelings of him possibly killing her after they were done, and it was an extremely eerie experience.

She couldn't sleep and hadn't had a decent night's sleep since his silent treatment began. Valerie considered just walking out and not coming back, but she thought of her family and their safety, and at this point she believed God heard her prayers and would protect her. While she was struggling to come up with a plan to leave him, she made the decision that she had to put her life in God's hands. She had finally reached the point where she was done with him and this toxic relationship that she had allowed herself to be in. She realized that he was not changing but getting worse if anything and that to love him more than she loved herself was not an option. She was done, the self-love was going to outweigh the toxicity that imprisoned her.

In a conversation with her mother, she assured her that she didn't believe there was anything to worry about,

"Mom, I know God is going to give me an escape plan, I trust and believe that. This is in God's hands now mom."

"I know we been praying Valerie, and I know God is able, but I'm still troubled a bit. This guy is really treacherous . . . and I don't trust the fact that he hasn't been speaking to you in the past two weeks."

"I know Mom, I know, and I feel impatient some time too, but right now waiting on God is our only safe option."

And trusting God is just what she did, along with leaning in on God and the hard part continued to be going from day to day not knowing what his move was going to be. She kept praying, fasting, and she asked God for His forgiveness every single day. This man had pushed her to a level she had never been on, to that place where you get to and there is nowhere else to go accept to God. Then the lonely world it created for her with no one to talk to. The pretense that shrouded her, it had been going on long enough, she wasn't sure how much more she could bear. What's worse, it often left her feeling extremely depressed. Still, she had learned to lean into God and with everything her faith to stay strong. She believed that God forgave her, and it was now her job to forgive herself—that would be the next great hurdle.

She thought often of the day she met Mike as she continued to ask herself *why did I ever give in and call him?* She was amazed how that one decision turned her life upside down. How she had gone from having a decent existence and a balanced life. One where she enjoyed the company of others and had a semblance of joy in her spirit to the point where she was now—feeling like a walking zombie, going through the motions of life but not physically aware of her surroundings, living in fear and anxiety all because of this toxic relationship that she was praying daily to get out of.

Three weeks into the silent treatment Mike was still giving her, she had him drop her off at her mom's house after work, as he did many times before. It was late and she asked her mom to take her home. After being dropped off, Valerie reached in her purse to get her house keys out to unlock the door. She tried to insert and turn her key, but the key didn't seem to fit. She looked at the lock closely and it looked dirty. Her lock was a shinning gold and that's when she then realized Mike had changed the locks.

She stared at the lock on her door in utter disbelief for about ten minutes. In the few moments she was standing at her door, her emotions where everywhere at the same time—hurt, betrayal, deceived, and angry all at once. She yelled, "He locked me out."

She continued to stare at the door, frozen in the moment, as the reality sunk in. Finally, she left the door, walked down the street to the nearest pay phone, and called her parents to come get her. Her mom arrived in twenty minutes and asked, "What happened . . . what's going on?"

"He locked me out of my own house. He changed the locks on me."

Valerie's mom was quiet for a moment then she exclaimed, "God has answered your prayers, you are free."

Valerie looked at her mom but didn't realize what she had spoken. It finally dawned on her—*God indeed made a way of escape for her.*

She joined in the praises with her mom. As they drove to her parents' home, she immediately felt an empowerment she had never experienced before, she thought *"Oh my God . . . God did it . . . I am free.*

Reflection

1. When Valerie finally made up her mind to leave Mike, she began to put herself first, she hadn't been happy for a long time and she knew that had to change.

2. Once she gave her toxic relationship over to God, she began to trust in Him and regained her power.

3. Valerie began to give herself back over to God and his principles, this gave her clarity of what real love was.

4. Mike's so called "silent treatment" was a time for her to see this was not a normal relationship, and that she was worth more than what he was giving her.

5. God gave her a way out of the relationship by the lock change. God knows us better than anyone, he used that along with her mom to set her free.

CHAPTER 11
THE AFTERMATH

esearch shows that domestic violence becomes heightened during the time of separation. It can potentially put the victim in life-threatening danger. (Source: Myths & facts about Domestic Violence Intervention Retrieved August 09, 2016). Women are 70 times more likely to be killed by their abuser after the breakup which is more than any other time of the relationship.

The night after Valerie came home and found her locks had been changed, Mike called her mom's house.

"When are you coming home?"

"How can I come home? You changed the locks," she replied.

Mike made up an outlandish story as to why the locks had been changed and tried to stress that he didn't try to lock her out. She didn't believe him—it was another one of his twisted mind games—but this time it backfired on him. She just knew she was free and would not be back as she felt God had answered her prayers and her faithfulness.

The events that followed her first day of freedom were mind blowing There were threats, stalking, emotional bullying and more. Valerie was in for a year of sheer terror, loneliness, abandonment, little to no help from law enforcement and the events that would take were unimaginable.

Mike became enraged when Valerie wouldn't comply with his wishes for her to come back to him. He called her several times and demanded that she return home and each time she told him no

He became so angry he yelled and told her, "Dammit . . . you'll come, or I'll come over and pick you up."

And then he was on his way to pick her up.

In the meantime, her mother told her to call the police. Valerie knew that was her only hope but she was still reluctant to do it.

A call to the police was no real help and was actually discouraging to Valerie at best. With some more coaching from her mom, Valerie relented, walked to the phone, and dialed the precinct. The dialogue with the dispatch operator and Valerie seemed to go on for about five minutes, maybe three minutes and two minutes was Valerie's reluctance to press the final digit on the phone.

Within a few moments, an officer was on the other end. Valerie took a breath and spoke.

"Listen . . . he's been abusing me and threatening my family and I have finally broken away, and he is threatening to come to my parent's home and get me. I need protection from him."

The officer listened intently but it seemed like the law was not on her side.

"Well ma'am, the problem with that is, is that we can't do anything to him for just saying what he is going to do and plus, we'd actually have to hear him say it."

Once again, she tried again to explain to the officer that her and her family's lives was in danger.

The officer continued, "Unless we hear him ourselves, we cannot arrest him."

She hung up the phone in frustration of what transpired. Shortly after there was a knock at the door.

It was Mike.

He asked for Valerie.

Through the door, Mary shouted, "No, you cannot talk to her."

A commotion between them ensued as he yelled Valerie's name from the top of his lungs. He was so loud the neighbors started to gather around. Valerie was embarrassed and felt horrible that she brought trouble to her parents' home.

The following Tuesday, Valerie had been dreading going to get her belongings from their place. She didn't want any more trouble from him and decided to call the police to go with her to place and they agreed to meet her there.

This was about three days after he locked her out and she grew tired of washing out and wearing the same clothes. Valerie knocked on the door with trash bags in her hands to get all of her belongings.

She motioned for one of the officers to go into the bedroom with her and what she found when she opened the closest almost caused her to faint. She felt lightheaded as she gazed in an empty closet. She whirled around and stormed into the living room where she found him sitting on the sofa.

Where are all of my clothes, shoes, jackets . . . where are my things?"

He was smug but still gave her a look of confusion and said, "I don't know."

Valerie began to cry. He had taken everything she owned, and she couldn't believe it. The officer told her she could file a civil suit in court, but there was nothing more they could do. The officer then pulled her aside.

"Why were you with a man like him. He has a rap sheet as long as your arm, and several aliases. You know he has a case, right?"

She nodded as the office continued.

"We've been after him for years, but we never have enough evidence to keep him because the witnesses never show up. We know he's killed a lot of people in the drug game and just on the streets . . . he's bad news."

The officer suggested she get a restraining order as soon as possible and continued. "We don't want anything to happen to you or your family because without that, you have no legal protection."

After that, Mike's behavior escalated as stalked her. Every morning she saw his car parked on her job's street. Her parents took her to and from work. Even though it humiliated Valerie, this is where she had to be for now. On the fifth day of his stalking, she and her mom went to the market. Valerie glanced into an unknown car next to her—it was Mike. He was really trying to get her, but her parents wouldn't let her out of their sight.

It got so bad to the point Valerie said, "Maybe I should just go back and deal with it"

Her mother was shocked. "You go back, and he will kill you . . . I can't let you go. I'll never see you again alive."

Valerie called the police again, and again they suggested getting a restraining order. When Valerie got to work the next day, she didn't see his car parked down the street. She felt maybe he had gotten the message and she actually laughed. She was even free enough to enjoy work and have a good time with her co-workers.

Later that day a tall man walked into her office with the biggest bouquet of balloons and flowers. Valerie knew they were for her but when a co-worker pointed in her direction, fear gripped her heart. Mike was a known killer, and she didn't know if he had hired the delivery guy to kill her, or if there was a bomb in it.

As he got closer to her, she said, "No . . . I don't want them"

He looked puzzled.

She noticed her co-workers looked afraid.

The next day while Valerie was getting ready for work, she received a call from her boss who basically said she wanted her to take some time off until she gets the restraining order. Valerie's co-workers were concerned with her behavior with the arrival of yesterday's balloons and flowers.

Valerie called her friend Staci and let her know she had finally left Mike. She reached out to her because she knew she could relate. Valerie asked her to take her to the courthouse to help her get the restraining order.

It was an all-day ordeal to get the restraining order, but she was happy. Mike never showed and the order was awarded for three years but she feared what would happen after Mike was served. Though surprised and relieved, she had not heard anything from.

Valerie's dad noticed Mike's car down the street the next morning and it seemed he was back to playing mind games. Valerie and her mom ran a few errands and, again, Mike was in the lane next to them about three cars down. Valerie broke into tears and cried, "How long is this going to go on?"

Mary did her best to encourage Valerie

"God has not spared your life this long to leave you now. Trust God."

Valerie knew she didn't have faith like her mom, but she was doing her very best.

Her mom asked, "When have you last eaten?"

Valerie couldn't remember when she last ate for she didn't have an appetite.

"You need to eat, Valerie, your clothes are getting loose on you."

She had been at her parents' house for about two months now and she had lost about twenty pounds because she simply couldn't eat due to the fear, worry, and stress of it all. Valerie had to serve Mike the restraining order and she prayed he would be as calm as he was the first time.

He wasn't.

Mike came to her parent's house and banged on the door. He demanded she come talk to him but, her mom told him no. He became so angry he picked up chair and through it at the door. She told him to stop, declared she had a restraining order in hand, against him, and that she was about to call the police.

He left but after that day he continued to stalk her, but it was if he was always within the limits of the order. It bothered Valerie and, she concluded this was not his first restraining order received. Valerie made sure she added all the names of her relatives and friends on the restraining order. She was so embarrassed she was passing out the orders like candy, she was worried he would harm them or have it done. Valerie tried her best to be happy as her parents told her she should. It was difficult due to the humiliating and embarrassing results of her poor choices, and now being back home with her parents, all of this had her feeling like a total failure.

She had returned to work and was glad for that, but she noticed a difference there, too. Her boss was a little distant and her co-workers looked at her strangely now. She thought it was the delivery incident, at first, but then noticed every time she talked to someone her boss would move them away from Valerie.

The main thing that hurt her was one of her co-workers mentioned she was sorry that Mike had stolen all of her belongings. Valerie felt the burn of betrayal go all though her. She had trusted and confided in her boss and now, she told her business. She was hurt and felt alone as her world had tumbled and she was headed into depression.

Valerie shared what happened at work with her mom, who subsequently tried to console her. She also suggested that Valerie get into counseling.

"Maybe it's time . . . Valerie . . . didn't the court suggest that when you got the restraining order, that counseling might be the way to go to help you process all of this?"

The court had given her counseling resources, and Valerie knew she needed the help but, still didn't feel comfortable sharing her business with strangers.

Still, Mike continued to stalk Valerie. On this particular Sunday she went to church and was in a pretty good mood for a change. She was on the lookout for him because for the past three Sundays, she saw him parked across the street. She did try and get a restraining order for her church, too, but the court denied it because it was a public place.

She shared with her pastor, whom she loved, what was going on and she felt bad because she didn't want to cause harm to anyone at her church. After bringing him up to speed, he assured her God would take care of her and the church. She felt a little uneasy, but she did enjoy the service.

Going into the sixth month of the breakup with Mike, he was still stalking, calling, and threatening her and it was exhausting. Valerie thought he would have given up by now as she was a nervous wreck. It was a chore for her to get out of bed every morning.

Valerie saw the restraining order wasn't working because it seemed he was always two steps ahead of the police. She was praying every day and waiting patiently for her prayers to be answered.

After a while she thought about getting counseling as the court suggested and soon after made her first appointment. The closer it got, the more nervous she would become as she contemplated whether to cancel her appointment. She wasn't sure if she'd be able to disclose the trauma. However, she quickly changed her mind after an eerie encounter with Mike that morning. It was now close to eight months of their breakup and he was still calling and begging her to come back. She nor her parents hadn't seen him in a while, but she saw him this morning after she had declined her mother's offer to drive her. As she walked to work, Valerie noticed he was parked near her job. Even though she was tired of being a burden to everyone, she wished she had of taken her mother up on her offer.

He didn't speak to her, but he just watched her walk by and had an evil smirk on his face. It was very scary.

Valerie felt her appointment with the therapist was a success, she discussed things that happened in her childhood, her abuse and abandonment issues she had from her biological mom and other issues that negatively impacted a healthy mental state. She shared how she knew her parents loved her, but she wished they had told her more often. She discussed how the lack of attention she didn't get as a child could've been the reason for her clinginess in relationships.

The therapist was helping her to resolve things from her childhood, and to eradicate her adulthood insecurities, or at least manage them. Valerie met with her therapist twice a week. She was learning to love herself and to put her needs and desires first, something she'd never done before.

In an effort to really focus more on her spiritual life, she joined the choir at her church, and helped with other auxiliaries. She regained her relationships with the members and joined some of the social clubs. Life was changing for the better as she was regaining her friendships and going out more and living. Valerie hadn't seen Mike in a little over a week but, she made sure her copy of the restraining order stayed in her purse just in case.

Entering the ninth month of the breakup, she felt life was good and then it happened—she saw Mike at the supermarket. Valerie had to pick up a few items for dinner, she went to the produce section, she was bagging up her food when she heard a voice behind her.

"How are you"?

She knew that voice and she froze. It was difficult to move, but she slowly turned around and was looking into Mike's eyes. He looked unkempt like he hadn't had any sleep lately.

She found her voice.

"How dare you talk to me . . . you've put me and my family through hell."

And in an instant, it was like he vanished into thin air. She left the store immediately but couldn't find him anywhere. That was the last time she saw him in person.

Over the rest of the year the calls continued, as he begged for her to return and every now and then she saw him parked in his car. Over time, however, all these incidences began to subside, and her confidence grew, and she became better and stronger. More importantly, she continued to give God the praise because she could admit things were getting better, and at last, she knew Mike was finally getting the message.

Reflection

1. Valerie is now free from Mike; her mom was the most influential person in her life.

2. Mike played one mind game too many by locking her out of her own home.

3. There were no stalking laws until the early nineties, Valerie would have had more support with those in place.

4. Valerie's childhood baggage of abandonment and neglect played a major role in the negative choices she made concerning the relationship with Mike.

5. Valerie is moving in a positive direction with her future, her faith, counseling and supportive family & friends are making this possible.

EPILOGUE

There is a saying that life isn't fair, unfortunately Valerie could relate to this too well. She had a troublesome childhood with issues ranging from all types of abuse and neglect. She learned to forgive and make the best of it, she tried to make it work, but didn't really master the art of "letting it go."

She became a born-again Christian at a young age and these Godly principles are what ultimately saved her sanity and life. Valerie knew counseling would benefit her, but she had put it on the back burner for a later time. And ended up taking all of her unresolved issues and baggage into a relationship with a total stranger, not realizing that her lack of "mother love" would make her a perfect candidate for an overbearing, manipulating man like Mike, who had his own insecurities.

There were many valuable lessons she took away from her experience with the domestic violence she endured with Mike. First was the absolute necessity of getting to know someone well before starting a relationship with them, especially an intimate one. Next, to not fear asking questions about their childhood, and endeavors that they have in life. Don't disclose any negative things or experiences of your past, let things grow naturally, then build up to what you share, and notice when the "sharing" is not mutual. Get to know their friends and family members as soon as possible. Get to know them. It could cost you your sanity and more importantly your life. Valerie has now learned how to work on her issues through prayer, counseling, and establishing healthy relationships, and allowing God to be the center of her life.

The main purpose of Valerie writing her story was to help anyone going through any type of abuse, whether it is with family, intimate partner, or whomever.

Love of self is the most valuable tool you have to protect yourself from falling prey to the kind of relationship Valerie found herself in. Too often women don't know how to do that because we are raised, and trained to be givers, to take care of others. If you don't know how to love and forgive yourself, seek help, through professional services, a spiritual leader, or whatever best suits you. You are worth it.

Valerie is not by any means perfect but, she's learned how to be the best version of herself by recognizing her needs, and by ceasing to hold everyone else in higher regard than herself.

AFTERWORD

PERSONAL EMPOWERMENT—The following are some suggestions that if followed can help you take ownership of your personal well-being. At the end of the day, no matter what situation we find ourselves in, we are responsible to first and foremost seek God's support as we act on our behalf, but to be intentional in not ever giving away our power—especially in matters of domestic violence.

By cultivating, maintaining, and sustaining a healthy sense of self, we prepare ourselves to recognize when we are in a manipulative and toxic situation. And we value our self and our time enough to leave it right away instead of making excuses for staying—we trust our instincts, and we trust God to direct us to relationships that are healthy and winning.

ACTION STEPS TO CULTIVATING YOUR PERSONAL EMPOWERMENT

You can begin to journal to help stay on track—start out slow and build up:

For the next 10 days write down your thoughts on the conscious changes you are making to better yourself. Below are 10 thoughts you can use to implement this strategy.

1. Do you put the needs of others before you? Start out by stating "I'm putting myself first"—What are the things you can do to put myself first.

_____

_____

_____

_____

2. Every morning when you wake up, try to give yourself the first five minutes for prayer, meditation, and self-reflection.

3. Remind yourself daily "I am good enough." No matter what flaws or shortcomings you have, remember you are good enough, you matter, and are as important as the next person.—No one is better than you.

4. Remind yourself you are here for a reason and you
    are no accident—Contemplate your purpose.

*"For we are God's handiwork, created in Christ Jesus to do good
works, which God prepared in advance for us to do"*
—Ephesians 2:10, NIV

5. Remind yourself, your past does not determine
    your future. Every day brings about a change. And
    each day is a new opportunity to fix it or get it
    right—It is healthier to keep focus on the future—
    not the past.

*"Yet you, Lord, are our Father. We are the clay, you are the
potter, we are all the work of your hand"*
—Isaiah 64:8 (KJV)

6. I will work on the things I can change & accept
    those that I can't—

*"Therefore, we do not lose heart. Though outwardly we are
wasting away, yet inwardly we are being renewed day by day.
For our light and momentary troubles are achieving for
us an eternal glory that far outweighs them all. So, we fix our
eyes not on what is seen, but on what is unseen, since
what is seen is temporary, but what is unseen is eternal."*
—2nd Corinthians 4:16-18 (NIV)

7. Reminder: Take 10-20 minutes every day to focus
    on yourself—it could be soaking in the tube with
    bubble bath, it could be a quiet walk, or reading

something you enjoy, put in an exercise tape and work on your body.

> *"Because you are precious in my eyes,*
> *and honored, and I Love you".*
> —ISAIAH 43:4 (NIV)

8. Reminder. You have the power to make this the best day that you can.

9. Reminder: Commit daily to making a conscious effort to work on your health.

10. Reminder: Try not to go into any new day with grudges from the previous day. Forgive others for their offenses to you and forgive yourself every moment you spent in a negative space.

Above all remember you are never alone. As soon as you feel it, seek help. See resources below and know "that the battle is not yours/no matter what you are going through/remember God just wants the chance to use you/remember *The Battle is Not Yours—It's the Lord's*. – lyrics by Yolanda Adams

RESOURCES

1736 Family Crisis Center
Los Angeles Ca, 90018-1353
Phone number:
Crisis line (213) 745-6434
Crisis line (213) 222-1237
Crisis line (310) 370-5902
Crisis line (310) 379-3620

A Community for Peace
Citrus Heights Ca, 95616
24-hour crisis line (916) 728-7210
LGBTQ Services (916) 736-2443
Main Office (916) 728-7210

Deaf Women's Advocacy Services (ADWAS)
Video phone 855 812-1001
Instant messenger: Deaf Hotline

Valerie completed this manuscript in October 2020, in the time of a Global Pandemic. The world is being affected by the Coronavirus or COVID-19. This time was challenging for the world at large where individuals were having to find ways to navigate through this "New Normal." Valerie diligently worked to complete this work. As she was working from and it was clear that during the shutdown, people were even more likely to be dealing with domestic violence. Her heart went out to them. She felt it was her duty to get this book published to be of assistance to others.

CPSIA information can be obtained
at www.ICGtesting.com
Printed in the USA
FSHW021728260721
83511FS